THE GUYS' GUIDE TO MAKING SPORTS MORE AWESOME

BY ERIC BRAUN

CAPSTONE PRESS
a capstone imprint

Edge Books are published by Capstone Press,
1710 Roe Crest Drive, North Mankato, Minnesota 56003
www.capstonepub.com

Library of Congress Cataloging-in-Publication Data
Braun, Eric, 1971–
The guys' guide to making sports more awesome / by Eric Braun.
pages cm.—(Edge books. The guys' guides)
Includes bibliographical references and index.
Summary: "Describes various tips, activities, and useful information for making sports
more fun and interesting"—Provided by publisher.
ISBN 978-1-4765-3921-8 (library binding)
ISBN 978-1-4765-5969-8 (ebook pdf)
1. Sports—Juvenile literature. I. Title.
GV705.4.B73 2014
796—dc23   2013035406

Editorial Credits
Aaron Sautter, editor; Veronica Scott, designer; Eric Gohl, media researcher;
Jennifer Walker, production specialist

Photo Credits
Alamy: North Wind Picture Archives, 28 (bottom); AP Photo: 18 (right), Gene Puskar,
20 (bottom); Capstone: 9 (bottom), 14 (bottom), 16 (left), 17 (all), 27 (bottom), Fernando
Cano, 15 (all); Courtesy of artofmanliness.com: 7 (illustrations); Dreamstime: Martin
Ellis, 24 (right), Naci Yavuz, 25 (left), Scott Anderson, 19 (bottom); Getty Images: Elsa,
21 (top); iStockphotos: Mike Rodriguez, 6 (top); Newscom: EPA/John G. Mabanglo, 23
(bottom left & bottom right), Reuters/Darren Staples, 7 (top), Reuters/Doug Kapustin,
6 (bottom); Shutterstock: 1973kla, 2 (buildings), Aleks Melnik, 2 (boxing glove &
popcorn), 12 (left), 13, 18 (left), Anthony Correia, 24 (left), bioraven, cover (top right),
4, CoolR, 28 (top), hjakkal, 23 (basketball hoop), JSlavy, 14 (top), Kaliva, 22, Kathy
Gold, 29 (bottom right), khandisha, 8 (bicycling gear), 9 (top left), 10 (bicycling gear),
11 (top), kstudija, 8 (silhouettes), LHF Graphics, cover (bottom), 25 (right), locote, 5, 10
(bicyclist), mhatzapa, 20 (top), 26 (top), mir_vam, 9 (top right), Mitch Gunn, 19 (top),
Mur34, 21 (bottom), Neyro, 23 (basketball), ranker, 26 (bottom), 27 (top), Rednaxel, 16
(right), Sergeypykhonin, 12 (right), Voropaev Vasiliy, 29 (bottom left), Yu Lan, cover
(top left), 2 (skate), zeber, 11 (bottom); Wikipedia: Mahanga, 29 (top)

Design Elements
Shutterstock

Printed in the United States of America in Stevens Point, Wisconsin.
092013   007768WZS14

TABLE OF CONTENTS

BE YOUR OWN SPORTS HERO!

Across the court, your opponent is bent over and breathing hard. It's been a tough battle. But when your eyes meet his, he gives you a smile. His team is up by three points. He thinks they've got it in the bag. Your teammate passes the basketball inbounds to you. You turn toward the basket with only six seconds left on the clock. What do you do?

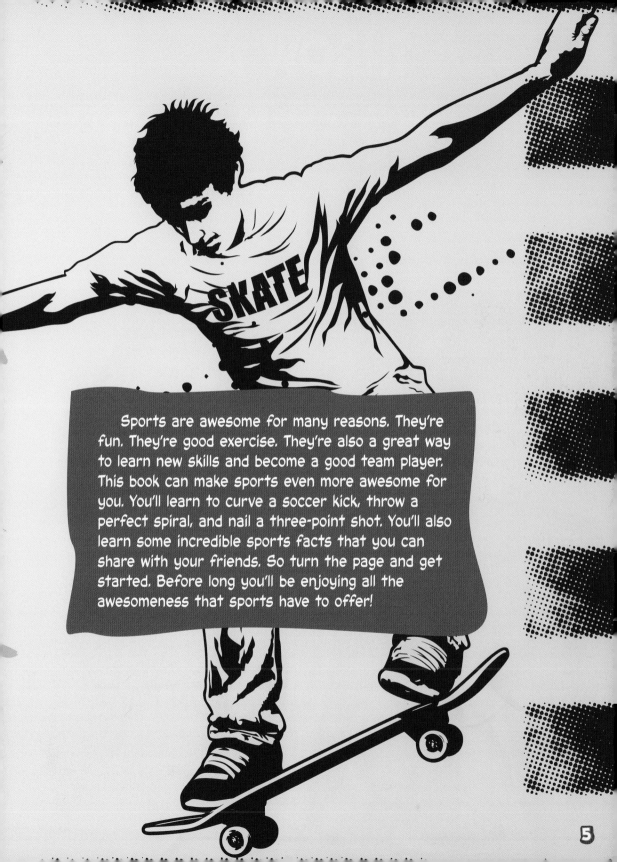

Sports are awesome for many reasons. They're fun. They're good exercise. They're also a great way to learn new skills and become a good team player. This book can make sports even more awesome for you. You'll learn to curve a soccer kick, throw a perfect spiral, and nail a three-point shot. You'll also learn some incredible sports facts that you can share with your friends. So turn the page and get started. Before long you'll be enjoying all the awesomeness that sports have to offer!

THROW A
DAZZLING KNUCKLEBALL

The batter takes a swing—and misses! A well-thrown knuckleball is very difficult to hit. In a knuckleball pitch, the ball barely spins after you release it. Air pushes the ball in different directions so it wobbles as it floats toward the batter.

1 Grip the ball with your thumb on the bottom and your fingertips on top. Place your fingertips against the horseshoe-shaped seam in the ball.

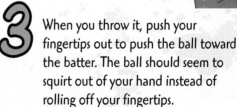

2 Wind up as if you are going to throw a typical fastball. Keep the ball hidden in your glove for as long as possible. You don't want the batter to see how you're holding the ball.

3 When you throw it, push your fingertips out to push the ball toward the batter. The ball should seem to squirt out of your hand instead of rolling off your fingertips.

FUN FACT:

Major League Baseball (MLB) pitcher R. A. Dickey won the National League Cy Young Award in 2012. Almost all of his pitches are knuckleballs.

THROW A
PERFECT SPIRAL

Footballs have an odd, oblong shape. It's easy to make wobbly passes that miss the receiver. Learn to throw a good spiral pass, and you'll have a better chance of hitting the target.

1 Hold the ball about two-thirds of the way back with your fingers on the laces. This will give you control and power on your pass.

2 Stand with your feet about shoulder-width apart. Hold the ball in both hands at chest level.

3 Step toward your target with your lead leg. Your non-throwing shoulder should also face toward the target. At the same time, bring your throwing arm back.

4 When you throw the ball, drop your lead elbow as you move your throwing arm forward. When you release the ball, your throwing arm should be fully extended toward your target.

5 The key to a great spiral is in the release. As you release the ball, snap your wrist down so your thumb points toward the ground. To create spin, let the ball roll off your fingers. The tip of your index finger should be the last thing to touch the ball. Keep practicing until you've mastered the art of a perfect spiral pass.

HOST A BIKE OLYMPICS

Take bike riding to the next level with a little competition. Gather your friends together to hold your own bike Olympics! You'll need a large open area, such as a parking lot. Try using the following events, or make up your own. Have fun, and be sure to always wear a helmet for safety.

SPRINT RACE

Choose a short distance, such as 150 feet (46 meters). Mark off the start and finish lines. When you race, take off as fast as possible and go all out until the finish line.

ENDURANCE RACE

Map out a long course through your neighborhood, or have riders go several laps around your block. The rider who completes the course in the fastest time wins.

OBSTACLE COURSE

Use traffic cones, rope, boxes, or chalk lines to make an obstacle course. Time each rider as he or she goes through it. The fastest time wins.

THE INCREDIBLE STING-RAY

Schwinn introduced the Sting-Ray bicycle in 1963. The Sting-Ray featured high handlebars, a banana seat, and a close wheelbase. Its design was different from previous bikes. Kids soon learned that the Sting-Ray was perfect for doing wheelies and bunny hops, as well as racing on dirt courses. The Sting-Ray eventually led to today's popular BMX bikes, races, and stunts.

PAPERBOY CONTEST

Hang a Hula-Hoop from a tree branch or some playground equipment. Riders score points by throwing tennis balls or rolled-up newspapers through the hoop as they ride by. If the score is tied, move the riders farther from the hoop.

BUNNY HOP CONTEST

Stand a piece of plywood upright on the ground. Then have riders hop their bikes as they ride past the board. Mark the height of each rider's jump on the board. The highest jumper wins!

BIKE POLO

This event requires a lot of skill and should be played only by experienced riders. Teams of three, four, or five compete on a grass field or parking lot. Riders hit a street hockey ball with a bike polo mallet to try to score points. You can order a bike polo mallet on the Internet. Or you can build your own mallet with a ski pole and a piece of PVC pipe. Get an adult to help you build the mallet. Use traffic cones to set up goals at each end of the playing area.

FIND A SPONSOR

You can make your bike Olympics an awesome public event by asking a bike shop to sponsor you. Use the bike shop's parking lot, or ask if they can set up the event at your local community center. Ask people from the shop to discuss safety equipment, safe riding tips, and bike maintenance. You can also ask for help organizing and advertising the event.

CREATE AN AWESOME FANTASY LEAGUE

Sports fans love dramatic buzzer-beaters and last-second touchdowns. But there's a way to make your favorite sport even more fun—start your own fantasy league! In fantasy sports, people pick pro players for made-up teams that they manage themselves. Points are scored based on league rules and how players perform in real games. Try these tips to help your league stand out.

TIP:

Consider starting a fantasy league based on an obscure sport. Why not try fantasy BMX, fantasy chess, fantasy fishing, or fantasy lacrosse? Some people even play fantasy curling!

POP CORN

Invite all your friends to join your league. People don't need to be big sports fans to enjoy running a fantasy team. Just enjoying some friendly competition is half the fun.

Include an unusual scoring category. Make things interesting with different scoring systems. For example, maybe your fantasy football team can get extra points for fake field goals. Or try taking away points for penalties.

Do a live draft at someone's house. Fantasy sports are about spending time with friends. Grab some snacks, break out your cheat sheets, and get ready for some good-natured heckling with your buddies.

Try an auction league. In an auction league, everyone has a set amount of imaginary money. Team owners track the money they spend on each player. Once the money is gone, they can't get more players. It takes a skilled owner to get the best players for the least money.

It's fun to give your friends a hard time during the season. But be careful not to go too far. Do it in the spirit of fun and friendship. Nothing kills the fun like mean comments that hurt people's feelings.

draft—an event in which players are chosen to join different sports teams

auction—a way of selecting players in fantasy sports; owners use imaginary money to bid on players they want on their team

CURVE A SOCCER KICK

During a **penalty kick** in soccer, you can make the goalie's job difficult with a curved kick. With enough practice, you can even curve the ball into the net on a **corner kick**.

1. Approach the ball from a 45-degree angle.

2. Plant your non-kicking foot a little behind the ball. Then swing your kicking leg at an angle that will bring it across your body during the follow through.

3. With the inside of your kicking foot, begin the kick at the bottom outside corner of the ball. Move your foot diagonally toward the top inside corner of the ball.

4. During your follow through, turn your shoulders toward your target so your leg follows across your body.

GETTING A GREAT CURVED KICK TAKES A LOT OF PRACTICE.

DON'T GET DISCOURAGED!

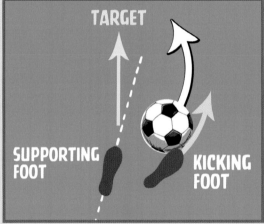

TARGET

SUPPORTING FOOT

KICKING FOOT

---

penalty kick—a free kick awarded to the offense when the defense commits a penalty

corner kick—a kick from the corner of the field; awarded to the attacking team when the defense kicks the ball out of bounds over the end line

OLLIE A
SKATEBOARD

Ollie-oop! Experienced skateboarders know how to do a simple jump trick called an ollie. This cool move will have you hopping your board over stuff in no time.

1. Place your back foot on the board's tail end. Keep your front foot at the middle of the board.

2. As you roll forward, crouch down slightly, and then jump straight up. Raise your arms when you jump.

3. As you jump, slam down the tail of the board with your back foot. The nose of the board will bounce upward.

4. While in the air, slide your front foot forward to level out the board. At the same time, lift your back foot so the tail of the board can rise.

5. Be sure to keep your knees bent to help cushion your landing.

FUN FACT:

Alan Gelfand invented the ollie in 1976 as a way to "get air" in empty swimming pools and skate bowls. In 1982 Rodney Mullen became the first skater to do an ollie on flat ground.

BUILD A SKATE RAMP

Learning skateboard tricks is fun, but it takes a lot of practice. You can use this runt ramp to practice small airs and lip tricks.

Be sure not to use power tools without an adult's help. If you get hurt, you'll be spending time in the hospital instead of on your skateboard.

SUPPLIES

- 1 sheet of 3/4-inch (1.9-cm) plywood, 4 x 8 feet (1.2 x 2.4 m)
- 2 sheets of 1/4-inch (0.6-cm) plywood, 4 x 4 feet (1.2 x 1.2 m)
- 1 sheet of 1/8-inch (0.3-cm) hardboard, 4 x 6 feet (1.2 x 1.8 m)
- 13 boards 2 x 4 inches (5 x 10 cm), 4 feet (1.2 m) long

- 1 box of 2-inch (5-cm) nails with wide heads
- 1 box of 2 1/2-inch (6.4-cm) wood screws
- hammer
- jigsaw
- drill with screwdriver attachment
- helpful adult

STEPS

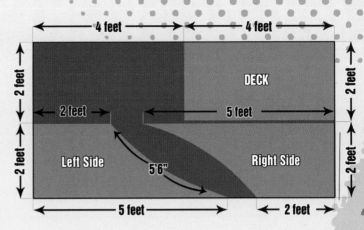

1. Mark out the two sides and deck of the ramp on the sheet of 3/4-inch plywood. Follow the measurements given here for each piece. Then with an adult's help, cut out the pieces with the jigsaw.

Left Side
Right Side
DECK

4 feet
4 feet
2 feet
2 feet
2 feet
5 feet
2 feet
2 feet
5'6"
5 feet
2 feet

2. Connect the two side pieces by nailing 2 x 4 boards between them. Start with the corners of the deck and the bottom of the ramp. Then nail the remaining 2 x 4 boards between the sides about 8 inches (20 cm) apart.

8" 8" 8"

3. Lay the deck piece on the support boards at the top of the ramp. Screw it into place along the outside edges. Be sure to always countersink the screws, making sure that the heads are below the surface of the wood.

4. Lay one sheet of 1/4-inch plywood into the curved ramp and screw it to the support boards. Then lay the second sheet of 1/4-inch plywood over the first and screw it down.

5. Finally, place the piece of hardboard onto the ramp and screw it down. It should overlap the end of the ramp and touch the ground. This will allow your skateboard to easily roll onto the ramp.

GREAT SPORTS MOMENTS

Sports fans love watching their heroes' incredible achievements. History is filled with stories of athletes who overcame nearly impossible odds. Here are a few amazing and inspiring stories every sports fan should know.

RUMBLE IN THE JUNGLE

One of boxing's most historic fights took place in Zaire, Africa. The 1974 match was nicknamed the "Rumble in the Jungle." The fight featured Muhammad Ali and George Foreman, who was the current champion. Many thought Foreman would win easily. However, Ali had a plan. He let Foreman unleash a string of huge punches, blocking most of them. Foreman soon grew tired. That's when Ali began landing his own punches. He knocked Foreman out in the eighth round. Ali later called his strategy the "rope-a-dope" method.

WEIRD WAY TO WIN

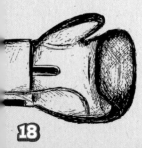

In a 1989 boxing match, light heavyweight champion Steve McCarthy had Tony Wilson up against the ropes. But then things got weird. Wilson's mom jumped into the ring and started whacking McCarthy with her shoe! McCarthy was cut on the head and unable to go on. The judges ended up giving the victory to Wilson.

PERFECT IN THE POOL

At the 2008 Summer Olympics, hopes were sky-high for American swimmer Michael Phelps. In the 2004 Olympics, Phelps had won eight medals, including six golds. He had also broken five world records. Everybody was talking about what Phelps might do in 2008. But if he was nervous, he didn't show it. He won all of his events and set a record with eight gold medals in a single Olympics. Phelps went on to add another six medals during the 2012 Olympics. With a total of 22 career medals, Phelps is the most successful Olympic athlete of all time.

RUNNING BACK ...
ALL THE WAY BACK

Near the end of the 2011 season, Minnesota Vikings star running back Adrian Peterson suffered a major knee injury. Doctors repaired it, but they didn't think he'd be ready for the start of the 2012 season. However, Peterson said that he would be ready—and he was! He rushed for 84 yards and two touchdowns in his first game back. He went on to become only the seventh player in history to rush for more than 2,000 yards. In fact, with a total of 2,097 rushing yards, he came just nine yards short of breaking the single-season rushing record! Peterson topped off his amazing season by winning the 2012 NFL Most Valuable Player award.

DEVASTATING

SUPER BUMMERS

Almost everyone enjoys some kind of sport. However, being a sports fan can be a lot like riding on a roller coaster. There are plenty of ups and downs. Check out a few of the biggest heartbreaks sports fans have dealt with over the years.

In 1991 the Buffalo Bills were big favorites to win Super Bowl XXV. But they lost the game when Buffalo kicker Scott Norwood missed his last-second field goal attempt. Losing that game was bad enough, but it was only the beginning. The Bills went on to become the only team in history to go to four Super Bowls in a row. But sadly for Bills fans, the team lost every time.

NO GOAL?

In 1999 the Buffalo Sabres were one game away from winning their first Stanley Cup title. But during the third overtime, Dallas Stars wing Brett Hull stuck his skate into the **crease**. He kicked the puck away from the goalie and then flipped it into the net. But when Hull scored, his skate was still in the crease, which was against the rules. However, the officials ruled that the goal was legal. To this day Sabres fans claim that Hull cheated to win the Stanley Cup. And Buffalo has still never won a championship.

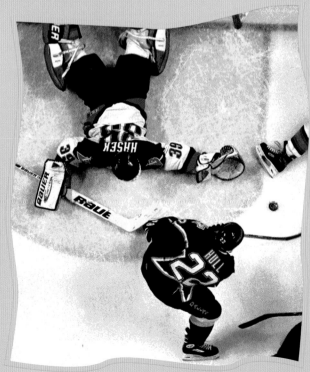

crease—the area directly in front of the goal in hockey

DISAPPOINTMENTS

FAN INTERFERENCE

The Chicago Cubs have not won a national title since 1908. And they haven't been to a World Series since 1945. But in the 2003 National League Championship Series, they were just five outs away from going to the World Series. In the eighth inning of game six, a Florida Marlins batter popped a long foul ball toward left field. As the ball sailed toward the stands, Moises Alou tried to catch it. But several fans reached out for it too. One fan, Steve Bartman, deflected the ball so Alou couldn't make the catch. The Marlins went on to win that game and game seven to go to the World Series. Many Cubs fans feel that "The Bartman Game" proves that the team is cursed.

THE CURSE OF THE BILLY GOAT

Cubs fans know a lot about curses. In 1945 a Cubs fan brought his pet goat into a World Series game. But he was kicked out because the goat smelled so bad. The angry fan declared, "Them Cubs, they ain't gonna win no more." The Cubs have not been back to the World Series since. The Curse of the Billy Goat seems to have stuck with the Cubs.

INCREASE YOUR RUNNING SPEED

The fastest runners in the world can sprint 100 meters in less than 10 seconds! You may not break any records, but these tips can help you increase your running speed.

1 USE GOOD FORM: Proper running form will help you achieve your best speed. Bend your arms at a 90-degree angle, and keep your hands open and relaxed. While running, lean forward slightly to keep your **momentum** going.

2 PUMP YOUR ARMS: While sprinting, pump your arms straight up and down. Don't swing them across your body.

3 STAY RELAXED: Focus on relaxing your jaw, shoulders, and hands to keep them from getting tense.

4 PRACTICE YOUR BURST: Kneel down on one knee with your other foot in front of you. Push off with your foot to burst into a 15-yard (13.7-m) sprint. Do this three times. Then switch your feet and repeat the process.

momentum—speed created by movement

NAIL A THREE-POINT SHOT

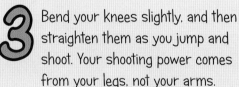

FLICK WRIST DOWN TO FOLLOW THROUGH

EXTEND SHOOTING ARM TOWARD BASKET

Your team is down by two points with only seconds left on the clock. If you practice the following tips, you can be a hero by nailing a last-second three-pointer.

1 It's hard to shoot the ball well if you're wobbly. Line up your body with the basket, and then practice keeping your balance by standing on one foot.

2 Cradle the ball with your fingertips, not your palm. Support the side of the ball with your non-shooting hand. Focus your eyes on the square above the rim on the backboard.

3 Bend your knees slightly, and then straighten them as you jump and shoot. Your shooting power comes from your legs, not your arms.

4 Extend your shooting arm and hand fully when shooting the ball. As you release the ball, follow through by flicking your wrist down. It should look like you're reaching for the rim with your hand.

AWESOME SPORTS DYNASTIES

BASEBALL

NEW YORK YANKEES

FOUNDED: in 1901 as an original member of the American League

WINNER OF: a record 27 World Series championship titles

WON: 10 championships between 1947 and 1962

FAMOUS PLAYERS: Babe Ruth, Lou Gehrig, Joe DiMaggio, Mickey Mantle, Yogi Berra, and Derek Jeter

MAJOR LEAGUE BASEBALL HALL OF FAME: includes 44 Yankees players and 11 managers, more than any other team

TEAM VALUE: more than $2 billion

HOCKEY

MONTREAL CANADIENS

FOUNDED: in 1909, it is the National Hockey League's (NHL) oldest team

WINNER OF: 24 championships, more than any other NHL team

WON: the Stanley Cup five years in a row from 1956 to 1960, the longest streak in NHL history

FAMOUS PLAYERS: Howie Morenz, Guy Lafleur, Larry Robinson, Jacques Plante, Doug Harvey, Jean Beliveau, Maurice Richard

TEAM VALUE: $575 million

dynasty—a team that wins multiple championships over a period of several years

Some fans love them. Other fans hate them. Few things stir up fans' passions more than debating sports dynasties. The following teams have a long history of success. Share these team facts and stats with your friends. Then ask them which team they think should be called the greatest dynasty of all time.

SOCCER

MANCHESTER UNITED

FOUNDED: in 1878

WINNER OF: 20 championship titles and 11 Football Association Challenge Cups (FA Cup)

WON: 13 Premier League titles between 1993 and 2013

In the 1998–99 season, won the Premier League, the FA Cup, and the Union of European Football Associations (UEFA) Champions League in one season

FAMOUS PLAYERS: Cristiano Ronaldo, Teddy Sheringham, Duncan Edwards, Denis Law, Eric Cantona, Bobby Charlton, George Best

TEAM VALUE: more than $3 billion

TOP TEAMS

TEAM	CHAMPIONSHIPS
NEW YORK YANKEES	27
MONTREAL CANADIENS	24
MANCHESTER UNITED	20
BOSTON CELTICS	17
LOS ANGELES LAKERS	16
GREEN BAY PACKERS	13
TORONTO MAPLE LEAFS	13
DETROIT RED WINGS	11
ST. LOUIS CARDINALS	10
CHICAGO BEARS	9
OAKLAND ATHLETICS	9

■ BASEBALL   ■ HOCKEY   ■ SOCCER
■ BASKETBALL   ■ FOOTBALL

PULL OFF THE HOOK-AND-LADDER

If you're losing a football game, you may need to try a trick play to get back in it. The hook-and-ladder may provide the spark the offense needs. Keep practicing until you get the timing down, and your opponents will never see it coming!

1. Two wide receivers line up next to each other on one side of the field.

2. The inside receiver runs faster and a little ahead of the outside receiver. At a set distance he turns, or "hooks," toward the inside of the field.

3. The quarterback throws to the inside receiver just as he breaks into his hook.

4. After catching the ball, the receiver immediately **laterals** the ball to the outside receiver behind him. With the right timing, the second receiver can streak toward the end zone without missing a step.

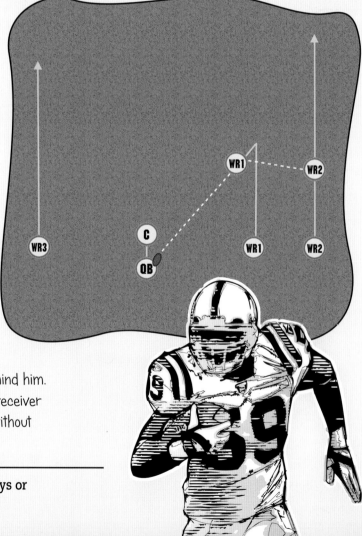

lateral—to pass the ball sideways or backward to another player

BLAST A
PING-PONG SERVE

In Ping-Pong, getting a good serve is an important part of the game. Here's how to put some spin on your serve to blast it past your opponent.

Topspin causes the ball to quickly shoot forward when it hits the opponent's side of the table.

1. Hold the paddle at a 45-degree angle facing downward. Start your swing below the ball.

2. Swing the paddle upward and away from you to give the ball forward spin.

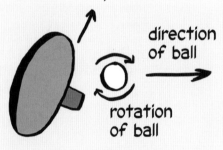

direction of paddle

direction of ball

rotation of ball

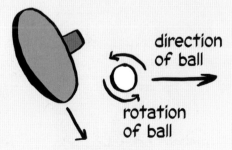

direction of ball

rotation of ball

direction of paddle

Backspin makes the ball slow down and drop sooner than your opponent expects it to.

1. Hold the paddle at a 45-degree angle facing upward. Start your swing from above the ball.

2. Hit the ball with an angled, downward swing to give the ball backward spin.

AN AWESOME ANCIENT STADIUM

THE COLOSSEUM

The ancient Romans enjoyed sports as much as we do today. But one sport was very different. In the gladiator games, warriors fought for their lives in gruesome, bloody battles. These men and women were usually prisoners of war and criminals. Their punishment was to fight to the death to entertain huge crowds.

Early gladiator games were often held in fenced fields and public squares. But none of these allowed many people to see the action. Soon the Romans invented the **amphitheater**—a circular stadium with tiered seating. This new design allowed fans a much better view of the action.

The Colosseum was opened in AD 80. It was the largest and most spectacular stadium of its time. It could seat up to 50,000 bloodthirsty fans, and every floor had bathrooms with running water. Fans could enjoy a variety of food and drinks and even buy souvenirs. Sometimes a play was performed between events, much like halftime entertainment at today's stadiums. Check out the chart below to see how the Roman Colosseum compares to today's AT&T Stadium near Dallas, Texas.

	THE COLOSSEUM	AT&T STADIUM
YEAR OPENED	80	2009
SIZE	615 feet (187 m) long, 156 feet (47.5 m) high	900 feet (274 m) long, 800 feet (244 m) high
CAPACITY	50,000	80,000; standing room for another 25,000
ROOF	A huge awning could be pulled across the seating area using pulleys and ropes.	A 14,000-ton (12,700-metric ton) retractable steel roof opens and closes in 18 minutes using electric motors.
SPECIAL FEATURE	A complex set of underground passages, cages, and rooms was under the arena where gladiators and animals waited to fight. The fighters and animals were sometimes lifted through trap doors in the arena floor for their matches.	A 600-ton (544-metric ton), four-sided video board hangs from the stadium ceiling. Each side features a 162-foot (49-m) wide, high-definition screen.

amphitheater—a large, open-air building with rows of seats in a high circle around an arena

GLOSSARY

amphitheater (AM-fuh-thee-uh-tuhr)—a large, open-air building with rows of seats in a high circle around an arena

auction (AWK-shuhn)—a way of selecting players in fantasy sports; owners use imaginary money to bid on players they want on their team

bunny hop (BUN-ee HOP)—a short jump done from flat ground on a bike

corner kick (KOR-nur KICK)—a kick from the corner of a soccer field; awarded to the attacking team when the defense kicks the ball out of bounds over the end line

countersink (KOUN-tur-sink)—to cause the head of a screw to sink below the surface of an object

crease (KREES)—the area directly in front of the goal in hockey

draft (DRAFT)—an event in which players are chosen to join different sports teams

dynasty (DYE-nuh-stee)—a team that wins multiple championships over a period of several years

lateral (LAT-ur-uhl)—to pass the ball sideways or backward to another player

momentum (moh-MEN-tuhm)—speed created by movement

penalty kick (PEN-uhl-tee KICK)—a free kick awarded to the offense when the defense commits a penalty

READ MORE

Doeden, Matt. *Play Football Like a Pro: Key Skills and Tips.* Play Like the Pros. Mankato, Minn.: Capstone Press, 2011.

Hetrick, Hans. *This Book's Got Game: A Collection of Awesome Sports Trivia.* Super Trivia Collection. Mankato, Minn.: Capstone Press, 2012.

LeBoutillier, Nate. *The Best of Everything Baseball Book.* The All-Time Best of Sports. Mankato, Minn.: Capstone Press, 2011.

INTERNET SITES

FactHound offers a safe, fun way to find Internet sites related to this book. All of the sites on FactHound have been researched by our staff.

Here's all you do:

Visit www.facthound.com

Type in this code: 9781476539218

Check out projects, games and lots more at
www.capstonekids.com

INDEX